AIVARAS GRAUZINIS

The Million Dollar Dialogue

Create Winning Ideas With ChatGPT

PHILEAS LIBRIS PUBLISHING

First edition

This book was professionally typeset on Reedsy.
Find out more at reedsy.com

Contents

Introduction	1
The AI Revolution Begins	1
The Power of Dialogue	3
The objective of the Book	4
Part I: Understanding AI and How to Talk To It	7
Basics of Artificial Intelligence	7
Large Language Models	9
So what is Prompt Engineering?"	12
And what is a prompt, to begin with?	12
Prompt Engineering	14
Brainstorming with AI	16
Part II: The Art of Prompting AI	19
"Understanding AI-Language and Responses"	19
"Crafting Effective Prompts"	21
Step 1: Define Your Objective	22
Specificity	23
Use of Simple Language	25
Spellchecking and Syntax Correction	27
Step 2: Prompt Construction	28
Constructing Structured Prompts	28
Encouraging Improvisation	30
Step 3: Building on Responses	32
Follow-Up Questions	32
Seeking Clarification and Details	33
Reminding for AI Objectives and Initial Tasks	35
Step 4: Challenging Assumptions	36

Questioning Assumptions 37

What-If Scenarios 38

Step 5: Divergent Thinking 39

Encouraging Divergent Responses 39

Giving New Roles for AI to Test Interesting Ideas 41

Step 6: Convergent Thinking 42

Narrowing Down Ideas 43

Synthesising Ideas 45

Expanding and Filling in Gaps 47

Step 7: Iterative Feedback 49

Iterative Refinement 49

External Feedback Integration 50

Step 8: Documentation and Reflection 51

Documenting the Process 51

Utilising AI for Summaries and Feedback 52

Creating "Cheat Sheets" of Prompts 52

Experimentation 53

Step 10: Interesting Hacks 54

Hack Yourself 54

Using Tags 54

Super-prompts 56

Part IV: What's Next? 59

Custom Instructions 59

GPTs 63

Conclusion 66

APPENDIX 69

Ideation Prompts 69

Brainstorming Prompts 71

Idea Screening and Evaluation Prompts 72

Market Research and Analysis Prompts 73

Analytic Prompts 74

Synthesising Prompts 75

Diverging Prompts 76

Action Prompts   78
Superprompts   79
Custom Instructions   85

Introduction

The AI Revolution Begins

In an era where technology relentlessly reshapes our world, nothing has sparked more intrigue and potential than Artificial Intelligence (AI). Gone are the days when AI was just a fanciful concept in science fiction. Today, it stands at the forefront of a revolution, fundamentally altering how we work, think, and interact.

And while we have all heard the term "AI" for quite a few years now, it has had little influence on our everyday lives, jobs, or opportunities. All sorts of industries, from automotive to health, from finances to agriculture, have that "AI" somewhere. But it is under the hood, out of our control, and most of the time, only means that things labelled with this "AI inside" will come at a higher price tag.

But then, on November 30, 2022, OpenAI released what they called "a low-key preview" called ChatGPT. Greg Brockman, OpenAI president, told his employees that day that it would not have much of an impact and would affect only the most specialised and interested people in the industry. Within the first few days, there were millions of subscribers, and this statement will go in history as one of the biggest understatements of the century. Because just a year later, most of our world changed.

This is, in fact, one of the biggest technological revolutions, comparable to, but I think, even bigger than the one Steve Jobs unleashed with his first iPhone.

At the heart of this revolution lies a simple yet profound concept: the division of success. The knowledge and ability to harness AI technology effectively are becoming the new dividing line, setting apart those who will thrive from those who will struggle to keep up. This division isn't just about who can use the most advanced technology; it's about understanding and leveraging AI to unlock potentials we never knew existed. And, for the very first time in the history of technological revolutions, everyone with internet access can participate and ride the way.

The marvel of this technology is that you do not need to be a technical guru, programmer, or mathematician to understand and use it. You do not need large capital investment to harness its benefits and make a good living out of it. All you need is an electronic device with internet access and a finger to type. Well, and this book, to make sure you do it right.

So what is so special about this technology that holds such a promise? What all the fuss is about? The answer is quite simple: this technology, which only requires you to type, can make you a leader of a team of advanced specialists in absolutely any field in the world working for you. And that team pretty much holds most of the knowledge of humanity. That is what is so special about it.

I am a creative person, I love to learn, and I love science. But I have to admit - I am absolutely horrible at programming, and while I do appreciate the power of math, I have to draw a line somewhere at the beginning of the calculus. Despite that, for many years, I owned and managed a company stuffed with scientists and programmers developing advanced technological solutions.

Those guys were translating my vision into actual working things, using their skills and knowledge. And let's face it, some of them were much more intelligent than me. Yet that team and their combined knowledge made my visions a reality and made me a rich man.

And now, with these new advances in AI, in those silly named "chatbots", the opportunity is there for everyone to have their own most intelligent and knowledgeable team to work for them. But, just like me in my company, one has to learn to talk to the team to make it happen.

In this book, "The Million-dollar Dialogue: Create Winning Ideas with ChatGPT," I will attempt to do exactly that, to show you how to talk to AI to make it a winning team, develop ideas for you and help you implement them to make you, dear reader, a success story.

The AI revolution has begun. It's time to join the conversation.

The Power of Dialogue

Dialogue has always been a cornerstone of human communication. From the philosophical discourses of ancient Greece to the boardrooms of modern corporations, exchanging ideas through conversation has fueled innovation and understanding. Oddly enough, dialogue remains the most powerful tool in the age of AI, too.

Why dialogue? Because it is through dialogue that complex philosophies are unravelled, intricate problems are solved, and creative ideas are birthed. Plato, one of the greatest philosophers, used dialogue as his primary method of exploring deep and complex concepts; he believed that dialogue was the beginning of everything great. The back and forth, questions and answers, is the engine that generates good ideas and shakes bad ones out.

AI might hold the keys to human knowledge. More than that, it holds the key to the pattern of human thought - and this is the most valuable asset to have. The dialogue with AI might give you a chance to get the right keys and unlock the idea you were looking for.

However, engaging in productive dialogue with AI requires skills. There were many scientific papers published last year in psychology and computer science magazines about odd issues arising from people attempting to communicate with machines using natural language. It turns out it is difficult to do it the right way.

AI chatbots are indeed designed to take a natural language as an input. But natural language, for humans, is more than only dictionary and grammar rules. We are used to nuances, emotional tones and other cues that prompt dialogue between humans. None of that works with the machine, causing communication issues.

Besides, not everyone is skilful at communicating and expressing thoughts and ideas to begin with. And that, in fact, is one of the problems that prevents many people from getting good results while working with AI.

The good news is that mastering a dialogue that would create outstanding results while working with AI is much easier than mastering communications with a wide variety of people.

The objective of the Book

"The Million-dollar Dialogue: Create Winning Ideas with CharGPT" is not just a list of instructions for you to type in. Our objective is clear: to give you the knowledge and skills to use AI as a tool for generating groundbreaking ideas.

AI's capabilities are vast, but its true power is unlocked only when used effectively. This book is your roadmap to mastering the art of AI dialogue, turning this complex technology into a skilful team that works for you.

The first step in our journey is to view AI as a tool. Much like a skilled craftsman uses a hammer or a chisel, we must learn to use AI with precision and purpose. It's about leveraging AI's strengths - its processing power, data analysis capabilities, and pattern recognition skills - to complement our human creativity and intuition.

The core of our objective is to teach you the art of prompting AI. A prompt is more than a question; it's a doorway to possibilities. We will explore techniques to craft prompts that guide AI to provide not just answers but insights, perspectives, and creative ideas. We will learn to navigate AI's responses, to read between the lines, and to steer the conversation towards productive outcomes.

Beyond individual prompts, building an ongoing dialogue with AI is crucial. This book will show you how to develop a conversational flow, where each interaction builds on the previous one, creating a synergistic exchange of ideas. It's about creating a partnership with AI, where the exchange is not one-sided but a collaborative effort towards idea generation.

Our ultimate objective is to empower you on your AI journey. This book will equip you with the tools, knowledge, and confidence to use AI as a partner in your creative and problem-solving endeavours. It's about moving beyond the fear and uncertainty surrounding AI and embracing its potential as a catalyst for innovation.

As we embark on this journey together, remember that the goal is not to become AI experts but to become expert users of AI. It's about understanding how to communicate with this powerful tool, to guide it, and to leverage its capabilities for generating ideas that can transform businesses, industries, and even the world.

In conclusion, "The Million-dollar Dialogue" is more than a book; it's a gateway to a new era of innovation and success. Through the art of prompting AI and building effective dialogue, we can unlock a world of possibilities. Join us in exploring this exciting frontier, where AI becomes not just a tool but a partner in our quest for groundbreaking ideas and solutions.

Part I: Understanding AI and How to Talk To It

Basics of Artificial Intelligence

Before we can learn to use AI effectively for our benefit, it is important to understand, at least at the very basic level, what it is and how it works. I promise to do this without getting into technical jargon or lengthy technical explanations. No cogs and wheels, just things you need to know.

For those of us who have no background in computer science and programming, AI looks like a fantastically sophisticated, intelligent system thinking and solving our problems. Well, nothing can be further from the truth. Yes, it is very sophisticated, and yes, it can solve problems, a whole lot of them. It's just that it is not thinking.

Artificial Intelligence is a poorly chosen and misleading name for these technologies. Let us be clear from the very start: there is no intelligence, artificial or otherwise, in this technology.

AI refers to machines designed to mimic human intelligence, processing information and making decisions or predictions. At the heart of modern AI is machine learning, where computers learn from data the same way a dog is learning to catch a ball.

One pivotal aspect of machine learning is neural networks. These are intricate algorithms modelled loosely on the brains of living creatures, designed to recognise patterns and make decisions. Just as a child learns to recognise a cat by seeing many different cats, a neural network learns from vast amounts of data.

In this specific example, a machine neural network would be introduced to a large amount of pictures of the cats. Those cats in the images initially would be labelled by humans, for example, by drawing a red outline around the cat and giving it the label "Cat". The machine would analyse those pictures, learning all the possible features it could extract from those labelled areas in images. Slowly, it would learn to recognise a cat in other, not labelled images, too. Eventually, it can become nearly as good as humans in recognising cats in images. But, and this is important, the machine still has no concept of a cat and what it is. It just learned to recognise the cat.

However, this technology evolves fast and spans from simple rule-based systems to sophisticated neural networks capable of deep learning. This progression has led to the emergence of Large Language Models (LLMs) like ChatGPT, which can interpret and generate human-like text. They differ from human understanding as they don't possess consciousness but simulate understanding by analysing patterns in data.

Current AI capabilities include language translation, image recognition, and predictive analytics, profoundly impacting sectors like healthcare, finance, and transportation. However, it's crucial to remember that AI is a tool guided by human input and objectives. It is an extremely powerful and sophisticated tool, and like any other tool, it will perform only as well as the person operating it knows how to use it.

Large Language Models

Large Language Models (LLMs) like ChatGPT and Google's Bard are at the forefront of AI's interaction with human language. These advanced models, trained on vast and diverse datasets, have the remarkable capability to generate, interpret, and respond to text with high accuracy. Their training involves analysing a plethora of texts, ranging from books and articles to online forums and social media posts. This extensive training allows them to recognise and replicate various language styles and formats.

The core of LLMs lies in their prediction capabilities. They determine the most probable next word or phrase in a sequence based on the patterns they've learned. This predictive power is not rooted in any form of sentient understanding or thinking but is purely statistical, derived from the data they were trained on. As a result, LLMs can craft responses that are coherent and contextually appropriate, mimicking human-like text generation.

One of the most significant applications of LLMs is in natural language processing (NLP), where they have revolutionised tasks like text translation, summarisation, and question-answering. For example, in language translation, LLMs can interpret the context and nuances of one language and accurately translate them into another, maintaining the original intent and tone.

However, LLMs are not without limitations. Their reliance on pre-existing data means they may replicate biases present in their training material. Additionally, they cannot draw on real-world experiences or emotions, which sometimes results in responses that lack depth or understanding of complex human emotions and social nuances.

Besides, the way LLMs are trained also affects their performance. Some models are fine-tuned for specific tasks or industries, like legal or medical language processing, enabling them to provide more specialised and accurate responses in these fields. Others are more general-purpose and designed to handle a wide range of topics.

Despite these limitations, the use of LLMs has become increasingly popular in various sectors. In education, they assist in creating learning materials and tutoring systems. In business, they are used for customer service chatbots, content generation, and data analysis. Their versatility also extends to creative fields, aiding in writing scripts, poems, and even composing music.

In understanding LLMs, it is crucial to recognise their role as tools. They are designed to augment human capabilities, not replace them. Effective use of LLMs involves understanding their strengths and limitations and leveraging them in ways that complement human intelligence and creativity.

As technology continues to evolve, so will the capabilities and applications of LLMs. They represent a dynamic and evolving field in AI, one that holds significant potential for shaping the future of human-AI interaction. The next part of this series will delve into the commonly available AI modules, exploring how they differ in their functionalities and applications and how they can be effectively utilised in various domains.

For now, the most accessible LLM models are Google's "Bard" and OpenAI "chatGPT". There are quite a few others on the market, too, similar in nature and capability, but these two are just the easiest to access for someone unwilling to waste their time exploring this tech. So, in this book, I will spend most of my time talking about chatGPT and every now and the Bard too. Although both of them are LLMs, they have significant differences and, hence, different applications too.

Google's Bard, leveraging the vast data pool of Google's search engine, provides an enhanced search experience by integrating AI capabilities. It can understand and respond to user queries, offering information that is not only relevant but also presented in a conversational format. This integration allows Bard to access a wide array of internet-based information, making it a potent tool for information retrieval and knowledge discovery. Most importantly, Bar has access to all the information available for Google, and that means the very newest stuff, too.

On the other hand, ChatGPT, developed by OpenAI, excels in its conversational abilities. It can engage in detailed dialogues, answer complex questions, and generate creative content such as stories, poems, or even professional emails. This versatility stems from its training on a diverse range of texts, enabling it to understand context and respond in a human-like manner. ChatGPT is widely used for various purposes, including educational assistance, content creation, and customer service support. But, unlike Bard, chatGPT knowledge is more limited by the data it was trained on. It still is a huge amount of it, but the newest data in it will be at least a year old. Of course, you can provide the newest data for chatGPT by giving it to read texts, websites, and even video links, but there are still some limitations.

These AI modules represent the growing trend of AI integration into everyday digital experiences. They showcase how AI can be used to enhance information accessibility, provide educational support, and assist in content creation. The difference in their core functionalities—Bard's integration with search engines for knowledge-based responses and ChatGPT's focus on conversational and creative tasks—highlights the diverse potential of AI tools in catering to different user needs.

Moreover, the development and widespread availability of such AI modules have implications for various industries. In the field of education, they can assist in personalised learning and tutoring. In business, AI modules like these are transforming customer service by providing instant, intelligent responses to customer inquiries. In the creative arts, they are being used to inspire and assist in the creative process, providing new perspectives and ideas.

The adaptability of these AI tools also demonstrates the rapid progress in AI technology. As AI continues to evolve, we will likely see even more sophisticated and specialised AI modules being developed, each tailored to specific tasks or industries.

This evolution of AI modules is not just a technological advancement; it's a shift in how we interact with information and technology. AI tools are becoming more like partners in our digital interactions, capable of understanding and responding to our needs in increasingly sophisticated ways. They are transforming the landscape of digital technology, making it more interactive, personalised, and efficient.

As we continue to integrate these AI tools into various aspects of our lives, it's important to understand their capabilities and how to utilise them effectively. This is where the concept of prompt engineering becomes crucial, as it is the key to maximising the potential of these AI modules. The next section will delve into the intricacies of prompt engineering and its pivotal role in harnessing the power of AI for practical and creative purposes.

So what is Prompt Engineering?"

And what is a prompt, to begin with?

In the world of Large Language Models (LLMs), such as ChatGPT and Google's Bard, a 'prompt' is the primary method through which users interact with the AI. A prompt is essentially an input or command given to the AI, guiding it on what kind of response or output is expected. This could range from a question seeking specific information to a request for creative content like a story or poem.

Prompts play a critical role in the functioning of LLMs. They act as the starting point for the AI to generate a response using the patterns and knowledge it has learned during its training. The effectiveness of an LLM in providing relevant and accurate outputs largely depends on the clarity and specificity of the prompts it receives.

When a user inputs a prompt, the LLM processes it by searching through its vast database of language patterns and structures. The model then predicts and generates a response that it deems most appropriate for the given prompt. This process involves complex algorithms that analyse the prompt's context, intent, and desired outcome.

The simplicity or complexity of a prompt can greatly influence the nature of the AI's response. Simple prompts might elicit straightforward, factual answers, while more complex or creative prompts can lead to elaborate and nuanced outputs. The ability of LLMs to handle a wide range of prompt complexities is a testament to their advanced natural language processing capabilities.

However, the interaction with an LLM is not a one-way street. The quality of the output is often directly related to the quality of the input prompt. A well-crafted prompt can lead to highly accurate and satisfying responses, while a vague or poorly structured prompt might result in irrelevant or off-target outputs.

Understanding the importance of prompts is the first step in effectively using LLMs. As we delve deeper into prompt engineering in the next section, we'll explore how to craft prompts that maximise the AI's potential, leading to more meaningful and productive interactions.

Prompt Engineering

Prompt engineering is a nuanced and strategic method of interacting with Large Language Models (LLMs) like ChatGPT and Google's Bard. While initiating a dialogue with an AI using a simple prompt is straightforward, the art of prompt engineering involves crafting prompts that are meticulously designed to steer the AI towards generating the most relevant, accurate, and useful responses.

At its core, prompt engineering is about understanding the capabilities and limitations of LLMs and using this knowledge to formulate prompts that maximise the AI's potential. This process goes beyond casual or spontaneous questions; it requires careful consideration of the language, structure, and intent of the prompt.

Simple prompts, such as asking for the weather or requesting a brief summary of a topic, typically yield straightforward responses. However, the real power of prompt engineering is evident when dealing with more complex requests. For instance, when seeking creative ideas, detailed explanations, or solutions to specific problems, the way a prompt is constructed can significantly influence the quality of the AI's response.

Effective prompt engineering involves several key aspects:

Clarity and Specificity: Clear and specific prompts help the AI understand the exact nature of the request, reducing ambiguity and increasing the likelihood of a relevant response.

Contextual Information: Providing context helps the AI tailor its responses more accurately. For example, mentioning that a business-related query is for a small start-up can yield more targeted advice than a generic business query.

Guiding the AI's Focus: Well-engineered prompts guide the AI's focus towards the desired outcome. This could mean asking multi-part questions, setting a particular tone or style, or specifying the type of information needed.

Iterative Interaction: Prompt engineering is often an iterative process. Initial responses from the AI can be refined through follow-up prompts, gradually steering the conversation towards the desired outcome.

Creativity in Prompting: Creativity in prompt construction can lead to more innovative and unexpected responses, which is particularly useful in brainstorming sessions or creative writing.

The distinction between simply "chatting" with an AI and employing prompt engineering lies in the depth and effectiveness of the interaction. Casual chatting with AI might suffice for basic inquiries, but for more complex tasks, well-engineered prompts are essential. They ensure that the AI's responses are not just accurate but also aligned with the user's specific goals and needs.

The field of prompt engineering is rapidly evolving, with researchers and users continually discovering new strategies and techniques. As AI technology advances, the potential for prompt engineering grows, offering more sophisticated ways to interact with and leverage AI for diverse applications.

In conclusion, prompt engineering is a vital skill for anyone looking to maximise the benefits of interacting with LLMs. By understanding and applying the principles of prompt engineering, users can transform their interactions with AI from simple conversations to powerful tools for information gathering, problem-solving, and creative exploration.

Brainstorming with AI

Brainstorming with AI, particularly with advanced Large Language Models (LLMs) like ChatGPT, is an iterative and dynamic process that leverages the power of dialogue and added instructions to achieve depth and innovation in ideas. This process involves an ongoing back-and-forth interaction where the user's inputs and the AI's responses continually build upon each other.

At the outset, the user presents an initial idea or question to the AI. The AI, using its vast training data and language processing capabilities, generates a response. This initial exchange sets the foundation for deeper exploration. The key to effective brainstorming with AI lies in the user's ability to guide the conversation, refining and redirecting the AI's responses through subsequent prompts.

As the dialogue progresses, the user can incorporate additional instructions or constraints to focus the AI's creativity and analytical skills. This might involve asking the AI to consider specific factors, explore alternative perspectives, or generate ideas within certain parameters. The iterative nature of this process allows for the gradual refinement of ideas, with each round of interaction bringing more clarity and depth.

The user's knowledge of how to structure prompts and interpret the AI's responses plays a crucial role in this process. By understanding the AI's capabilities and limitations, the user can craft prompts that effectively steer the conversation towards productive and innovative outcomes.

Moreover, the process of brainstorming with AI is not just about generating ideas but also about evaluating them. The AI can provide feedback on the feasibility, originality, and potential impact of different ideas, assisting the user in the decision-making process.

In essence, brainstorming with AI is a collaborative effort that combines human creativity and intuition with the AI's computational power and data-driven insights. It's a process that underscores the potential of AI as a tool for enhancing human thought processes, offering new ways to approach problems and conceive solutions.

Through this iterative and deep dialogue with AI, users can tap into a level of idea generation and refinement that was previously unattainable, opening up new possibilities in various fields, from creative arts to scientific research.

AI and Great Ideas

In the dynamic intersection of AI and creativity, the generation of ground-breaking ideas is witnessing a remarkable transformation. In creative writing, AI's role as a brainstorming partner opens a realm of possibilities for narrative exploration. Writers utilising AI delve into varied narrative paths, character arcs, and plot developments, enriching their storytelling and series planning with nuanced details and innovative ideas.

The impact of AI extends into the entrepreneurial world, where it serves as a powerful tool for market analysis and business strategy development. Small business owners, through AI-driven discussions, can identify niche markets, refine their marketing approaches, and tackle complex challenges. This is made possible by AI's ability to process and analyse large datasets, offering insights into market trends and consumer behaviour that might otherwise remain hidden.

The effectiveness of these AI interactions hinges on a deep understanding of AI principles and the skilful application of prompt engineering. Crafting precise and insightful prompts enables users to extract highly relevant and innovative ideas from AI systems. These ideas, when effectively applied, can transform into successful business strategies or influential creative projects.

This process is not about generating random thoughts but rather about guiding AI to produce targeted, pertinent solutions that align with specific objectives and challenges. The key is in directing AI's computational power to complement and enhance human creativity and strategic thinking.

AI's role in ideation has become a critical asset in various fields. For writers, it means access to a vast reservoir of ideas and stylistic suggestions, enriching their narratives and broadening their creative horizons. For entrepreneurs, AI becomes a strategic partner, offering insights that drive business growth and innovation.

In both creative and business contexts, the utilisation of AI for idea generation represents a blend of art and science. It combines the imaginative aspects of human thought with the analytical strength of AI. This synergy is creating new opportunities and redefining the boundaries of what's possible in creativity and business innovation.

As AI technology continues to evolve, its potential to foster creative and business breakthroughs grows. Understanding and harnessing this potential is key to unlocking the full spectrum of opportunities AI offers. With the right approach and tools, individuals and businesses can leverage AI to develop ideas that are not only innovative but also deeply resonant with their target audiences.

Thus, "AI and Great Ideas" is not just a testament to the current capabilities of AI but a roadmap for its future applications. It's a journey into harnessing AI's power to create, innovate, and revolutionise how we think, create, and do business. By mastering AI interactions through prompt engineering and strategic thinking, the path to generating million-dollar ideas and achieving success becomes clearer and more attainable.

Part II: The Art of Prompting AI

"Understanding AI-Language and Responses"

So now that we covered the basics, we need to understand and shape our conversation based on AI operational principles and limitations. We need to get into the intricacies of how AI, particularly Large Language Models (LLMs) like ChatGPT, processes and interprets prompts. The quality and clarity of the input language play a crucial role in determining the AI's response accuracy and relevance.

The input language is the bedrock of effective AI interaction. LLMs rely on the words and structure of the prompts they receive to generate responses. If the input language is riddled with grammatical errors or is ambiguous, the AI may struggle to understand the intended meaning, leading to irrelevant or incorrect responses.

Consider the example of someone asking a friend, "What should I do?" In human interactions, the friend might understand the context and background, thus providing a meaningful response. However, an AI lacks this contextual awareness. Without additional information, this question is too vague for AI to address effectively. It has no access to personal history or the specifics of the situation, which are essential for providing a tailored response.

More importantly, AI has only the means of the prompt as a way to get any information from you. In human communications, we use intonations, facial expressions, and body language to enhance communication and express what is important and what we want. None of that is available for AI, so it has to be clearly communicated in your prompt: what it is exactly that you want. Which part of it is most important to you?

This highlights the importance of clear and specific language when interacting with AI. Users must provide enough context and detail in their prompts to guide the AI towards the desired outcome. Ambiguity and unclear sentences can significantly hinder the AI's ability to produce useful outputs.

There are some typical problems when users without knowledge of the AI field communicate with AI. Users often perceive the chatbot as a truly intelligent, sentient creature and communicate with it that way. But this is not true; there is no intelligence behind it, only a very sophisticated pattern-matching machine. However, this machine has access to a vast amount of human knowledge, unlike a web search engine, which only looks for matching keywords in the text. This machine matches the patterns of your prompt with the patterns of this vast knowledge. That is how it works - the better patterns it has to work with, the better patterns would be returned.

On the other end, there are users who treat AI chatbots as a glorified search engine. They type a question, get an answer, and this is it. It works, but it is just marginally better than a simple web search.

To mitigate this, users should focus on constructing well-structured, grammatically correct, and context-rich prompts. This involves not just stating the question or request clearly but also providing any relevant background information that could influence the AI's response.

Understanding that AI is a repository of human thought patterns is a crucial element in mastering the art of prompting AI. This way, you can learn to coax genius-level ideas out of it and, indeed, create the million-dollar dialogue.

Our next step will be to learn exactly how to do it.

"Crafting Effective Prompts"

At its core, prompt engineering is about crafting queries or instructions in a manner that effectively guides an AI to generate desired responses. This is an art form requiring both creativity and precision, as the way a prompt is structured directly influences the quality, relevance, and accuracy of the AI's output.

A prompt is more than just a question or a command; it represents the starting point of a conversation or an inquiry. The construction of a prompt determines how an AI understands and interprets the request. This understanding is critical because AI rely on the input they receive to formulate their responses. If the input is clear and well-structured, the output is more likely to be coherent and on-point. Conversely, vague or poorly structured prompts can lead to responses that are irrelevant, off-topic, or even nonsensical.

The effective prompt engineering involves a deep understanding of the AI's capabilities and limitations. It's about knowing how to phrase questions and instructions in a way that leverages the AI's strengths while mitigating its weaknesses. For instance, a well-crafted prompt can help the AI to navigate its vast database of language patterns and knowledge in a way that efficiently retrieves and presents the most relevant information.

More importantly, prompt engineering is not just about getting the right answer but also about sparking creativity and generating insightful responses. When done correctly, it can turn a simple query into an engaging conversation, a brainstorming session, or a deep dive into a specific topic. It's about finding that sweet spot where the AI's computational power meets human creativity and curiosity.

So here are the steps to get you working.

Step 1: Define Your Objective

The initial and perhaps most critical step in your dialogue with AI, like ChatGPT, is establishing a clear and precise objective. The clarity of your purpose serves as a guiding light, shaping the direction and outcome of your interaction. It's the foundation upon which effective communication is built, ensuring that the AI's responses align closely with your needs.

When defining your objective, it's crucial to be as specific as possible. This specificity not only narrows down the scope of AI's responses but also enhances the relevance and applicability of the suggestions you receive. For example, if your goal is to generate business strategies, specify the kind of business you are focusing on. Are you looking at startups, small businesses, or large corporations? Each category will elicit a different set of responses tailored to the unique challenges and opportunities they present.

In creative endeavours, such as writing a novel or developing a screenplay, this principle is equally important. Instead of a generic request for story ideas, specify the genre – be it romance, science fiction, or mystery. Go further by defining the mood, setting, or character types you envisage. For instance, "I'm looking for a suspenseful sci-fi story idea set in a dystopian future, focusing on a protagonist who is a young rebel fighting against a totalitarian regime." Such a prompt provides the AI with a clear framework to generate ideas that align closely with your vision.

This principle of clarity extends to technical and academic inquiries as well. If you're seeking solutions for a technical problem, detail the specific issue, the context in which it occurs, and any constraints or requirements. For example, instead of asking for "ways to improve software efficiency," specify "methods to optimise memory usage in Android mobile applications under restricted processing power conditions."

The importance of clarity of purpose cannot be overstated. It influences the quality of the AI's responses, the efficiency of the dialogue, and, ultimately, the success of your endeavour. By being clear and specific about what you want to achieve, you empower the AI to provide focused, relevant, and actionable suggestions.

Moreover, a well-defined objective helps set the tone and direction of the conversation. It acts as a compass, keeping the dialogue on course, especially in complex or prolonged interactions. When the conversation starts to drift, referring back to the original objective can help realign the discussion and ensure that it remains productive.

In essence, clarity of purpose is about knowing what you want to achieve and communicating it effectively to the AI. It's the first step in a journey of discovery, exploration, and problem-solving with ChatGPT. By clearly articulating your goals, you lay the groundwork for a fruitful and efficient dialogue, leading to outcomes that are not only satisfying but also aligned with your original vision.

Specificity

Specificity in your prompts is the key to unlocking precise and valuable responses from an AI like ChatGPT. When you provide detailed and focused questions, the AI can hone in on the exact area of your interest, leading to more actionable and tailored advice. This specificity turns a broad inquiry into a sharp, targeted dialogue, ensuring that the responses you receive are directly relevant to your needs.

Consider the difference in responses you might receive from a vague prompt versus a specific one. A general question like, "How can I improve my business?" is so broad that it could lead to a wide array of responses, many of which may not be applicable to your particular situation. The AI could suggest anything from financial restructuring to social media marketing strategies, which, while potentially useful, may not address your most pressing needs.

On the other hand, a specific prompt, such as "What are innovative marketing strategies for a small eco-friendly clothing brand targeting millennials in urban areas?" immediately narrows the focus. Such a question guides the AI to consider your specific market segment, the nature of your product, and your target demographic. The responses will likely be more relevant, practical, and immediately applicable to your business scenario.

This principle of specificity applies across various fields and objectives. In technical fields, for instance, rather than asking, "How can I make my website better?" a more specific question like, "What are the latest user interface design trends for e-commerce sites focused on outdoor equipment?" will yield more focused and expert advice, tailored to the specific industry and website function.

In creative projects, specificity helps in shaping the direction and style of the output. For example, instead of asking for "ideas for a painting," specifying "ideas for a surrealistic painting depicting urban life in the future" gives the AI a clear direction and style to consider, leading to more targeted and inspiring suggestions.

The benefits of specificity are multifold. It saves time by reducing the need for back-and-forth clarifications. It increases the chances of receiving innovative and insightful responses that are directly applicable to your situation. Most importantly, it ensures that the AI's computational resources are focused on generating the most relevant and useful information for your unique needs.

Furthermore, specificity helps in building a more coherent and productive dialogue with the AI. Each specific prompt builds upon the previous one, creating a cumulative effect where the quality of the conversation improves with each interaction. This approach not only enhances the immediate outcomes of your dialogue but also contributes to a deeper understanding of how to effectively communicate with AI systems.

In summary, the specificity of your prompts is a powerful tool in guiding the AI's responses. By being detailed and clear about what you want to know or achieve, you pave the way for more focused, relevant, and practical solutions tailored specifically to your needs and objectives.

Use of Simple Language

The use of simple, clear language is a fundamental aspect of effective communication with AI systems like ChatGPT. This approach involves utilising short, grammatically straightforward sentences, which greatly enhances the AI's ability to understand and accurately respond to your prompts. Simple language cuts through the potential for misinterpretation and confusion, ensuring that your interactions are more productive and focused.

When prompts are laden with complex vocabulary, lengthy sentences, or convoluted syntax, there is a higher risk of miscommunication. The AI might focus on the wrong aspect of a complicated sentence or misinterpret the intent behind a complex question. For instance, a convoluted prompt like, "What are the myriad ways one could potentially enhance the efficiency of solar panel technology in regions with suboptimal sunlight exposure?" contains multiple layers of complexity – from the phrasing of the question to the technical specifics. This could lead to a broad range of responses, many of which might not address your actual need.

In contrast, simplifying this prompt to "How can we improve solar panel efficiency in areas with less sunlight?" makes your question clear and straightforward. The AI can focus directly on the core issue – improving solar panel efficiency in specific conditions – without being sidetracked by unnecessary complexities. This leads to more accurate, relevant, and actionable responses.

The benefits of using simple language go beyond just clarity. It makes your interactions with the AI more efficient, as less time is spent deciphering the intent of the prompts. It also ensures that the AI's computational resources are effectively utilised in generating responses that are directly relevant to your query.

Moreover, simple language is particularly advantageous when dealing with topics that are already complex or technical in nature. It helps in breaking down complicated concepts into manageable, understandable pieces. For example, in discussing advanced technological solutions or intricate business strategies, a straightforward prompt ensures that the focus remains on the substance of the issue rather than the complexity of the language used.

In essence, employing simple, clear language in your prompts is not about dumbing down your questions but about enhancing the precision and effectiveness of your communication with AI. This approach ensures that the dialogue remains focused, relevant, and productive, leading to outcomes that are more aligned with your goals.

Spellchecking and Syntax Correction

Utilising tools like Grammarly for spellchecking and syntax correction plays a crucial role in ensuring the effectiveness of your communication with AI systems such as ChatGPT. AI technologies interpret input very literally, meaning that any errors in spelling or grammar can significantly alter the meaning and direction of the response. Inaccuracies in your prompts can lead to responses that are off-topic, confusing, or entirely irrelevant to your intended query.

The precision of language is especially important in AI interactions because these systems rely heavily on the specific wording of your prompts to generate responses. A misspelt word or a grammatically incorrect sentence can drastically change the context or intent of a query. For example, mistakenly typing "waste production in industries" instead of "waste reduction in industries" can completely reverse the meaning of your request, leading ChatGPT to provide suggestions on increasing waste production, which is the opposite of your actual intention.

Correct spelling and proper syntax are more than just good writing practices; they are essential tools for clear communication. They ensure that your prompts are unambiguous, allowing the AI to focus on providing accurate and relevant information. This attention to detail is particularly important when dealing with technical or specialised topics, where a single misused term or poorly structured sentence can lead to a misunderstanding of the subject matter.

In addition to preventing misinterpretations, using spellchecking and syntax correction tools contributes to a more professional and credible interaction. It demonstrates attention to detail and a commitment to clear communication, which is vital in any professional setting. Whether you are seeking business advice, technical solutions, or creative ideas, clear and error-free prompts will always yield better and more reliable results from AI.

In summary, employing tools for spellchecking and syntax correction is a key practice in interacting with AI. It ensures that your prompts are clear, concise, and correctly interpreted, leading to more effective and efficient AI dialogues.

Step 2: Prompt Construction

Constructing Structured Prompts

The art of crafting effective prompts for AI dialogue revolves around a structured approach that breaks down your query into four critical components: the objective, the circumstances, the task, and the desired output format. This structured approach ensures that your interactions with AI are focused and clear and yield the most relevant and actionable results.

Objective: Defining the objective is about stating clearly what you aim to achieve with the prompt. It sets the direction for the AI's response, ensuring that the ensuing dialogue aligns with your goals.

Circumstances: Detailing the circumstances provides context to the AI, helping it understand the environment or conditions within which the response should be applicable. This includes any specific constraints, demographic information, market conditions, or technological settings relevant to your query.

Task: Outlining the task involves specifying what exactly you want the AI to do. This could range from generating ideas, providing analysis, and suggesting solutions to making predictions. Being explicit about the task helps AI focus its computational resources effectively.

Output Format: Defining the output format is about specifying how you would like the AI's response to be structured. Whether you need a list, a detailed explanation, a step-by-step guide, or a summary, this clarity helps in receiving information in a ready-to-use format.

Applying this structure to your prompts can significantly enhance the quality and relevance of the AI's responses. Here are five examples of well-formatted brainstorming prompts that follow this structure:

Example 1:
Objective: Generate innovative product ideas.
Circumstances: Small tech startup, limited budget, young adult demographic.
Task: Suggest five unique tech product concepts.
Output Format: List format with a brief description for each product idea.

Example 2:
Objective: Develop marketing strategies.
Circumstances: Launching a new health drink, targeting health-conscious consumers in urban areas.
Task: Propose four marketing campaign ideas.
Output Format: Summary of each campaign idea with key marketing channels.

Example 3:
Objective: Identify potential challenges.
Circumstances: Implementing remote working in a medium-sized company.
Task: List possible obstacles and solutions.
Output Format: Bullet points for each challenge with corresponding solutions.

Example 4:

Objective: Improve customer service.

Circumstances: Online retail, high customer inquiries, multi-lingual support needed.

Task: Suggest tools and strategies for efficient customer service.

Output Format: Table format categorising tools and strategies with pros and cons.

Example 5:

Objective: Enhance team productivity.

Circumstances: Software development team, tight deadlines, remote collaboration.

Task: Recommend techniques and tools to boost team efficiency.

Output Format: Ranked list based on effectiveness and ease of implementation.

By structuring your prompts with these four components, you guide the AI to provide responses that are not just relevant but also contextually aligned with your specific needs. This structure acts as a blueprint, ensuring that each part of your query is addressed comprehensively, leading to more effective and efficient AI-driven brainstorming sessions.

Encouraging Improvisation

Encouraging improvisation in your dialogue with AI, like ChatGPT, is a vital technique for unlocking creative and expansive thinking. By framing your questions to foster exploration, you invite the AI to venture beyond standard responses, tapping into a wellspring of innovative ideas and novel perspectives. This approach is especially powerful when seeking fresh solutions to complex problems or brainstorming for creative projects.

Open-ended questions are the key to this explorative dialogue. They create a space for the AI to generate diverse ideas without the constraints of rigid structures or predefined expectations. Prompts that begin with "What are some innovative ways to…" or "How might we improve…" are particularly effective. They signal to the AI that you are seeking originality and creativity, encouraging it to analyse and synthesise information in new and unexpected ways.

This method of prompting is not just about generating a high quantity of ideas but also about seeking quality and depth. It challenges the AI to consider multiple angles and possibilities, often leading to insights that might not be immediately obvious. For instance, a prompt like "What are some innovative ways to use AI in traditional farming?" pushes AI to integrate modern technology with age-old practices, potentially leading to groundbreaking agricultural solutions.

Here are five example prompts that encourage improvisation and expansive thinking:

"What are unconventional methods to improve employee well-being in remote work environments?"

"How might we use virtual reality to enhance educational experiences for high school students?"

"In what creative ways can small businesses leverage social media to compete with larger corporations?"

"What are some out-of-the-box strategies for reducing carbon footprint in urban transportation?"

"How could we reimagine healthcare delivery to improve access in rural areas?"

These prompts are designed not only to solicit a wide range of responses but also to inspire the AI to think more creatively, considering possibilities that may not be immediately apparent. This approach is invaluable for generating fresh, innovative ideas that can lead to significant breakthroughs in various fields.

Step 3: Building on Responses

Follow-Up Questions

Follow-up questions are essential in transforming a basic AI interaction into a rich, multi-layered dialogue. When engaging with ChatGPT, follow-up questions are not just about seeking additional information; they are about deepening the understanding of the ideas presented, exploring nuances, and uncovering hidden layers. This dynamic process allows for a more thorough exploration of topics and leads to more insightful and comprehensive responses.

For instance, if ChatGPT proposes a new product idea, probing further with specific questions can uncover aspects that might not have been initially considered. Asking about market differentiation, potential challenges in development, or target customer segments prompts the AI to delve deeper into the practicalities and implications of the idea. This not only enriches the dialogue but also provides a more rounded perspective of the concept.

These follow-up inquiries encourage ChatGPT to apply its vast repository of knowledge in a more focused and detailed manner. They help in identifying potential hurdles, exploring alternative scenarios, and considering the broader impact of the idea. For example, if ChatGPT suggests a strategy to increase online sales, follow-up questions could explore customer behaviour patterns, the effectiveness of different marketing channels, or the integration of new technologies in the sales process.

Here are five well-formatted follow-up prompts that can deepen the dialogue:

"You suggested using social media for brand awareness. Which platforms would be most effective for our target demographic, and why?"

"Regarding the proposed eco-friendly packaging, what are the cost implications compared to traditional packaging?"

"You mentioned telecommuting as a way to improve work-life balance. How can we address potential communication challenges in remote teams?"

"In the context of the new educational app, how can we ensure user engagement among teenagers?"

"Considering the expansion into the European market, what cultural factors should we consider in our marketing approach?"

These follow-up prompts are designed to build upon the initial responses from ChatGPT, encouraging a more detailed and thorough exploration of topics. They help in extracting maximum value from the AI's capabilities, leading to more nuanced and actionable insights.

Seeking Clarification and Details

In the process of AI-driven brainstorming and problem-solving, seeking clarification and more detailed information is crucial. While ChatGPT can generate a wide array of ideas and strategies, these initial suggestions may sometimes lack the specificity needed for practical application. By requesting further clarification or details, you transform broad concepts into tangible, actionable plans.

This step of probing deeper is essential for two primary reasons. Firstly, it helps in understanding the feasibility and practicality of the ideas. A concept might sound promising in theory, but without detailed information on implementation, costs, and resources, it's difficult to gauge its real-world applicability. Secondly, seeking details encourages a more comprehensive exploration of the subject, leading to a thorough understanding of the complexities and nuances involved.

For example, if ChatGPT suggests a new marketing strategy, it's valuable to ask for a step-by-step outline of how this strategy would be implemented in your specific business context. Questions about the estimated costs, resources needed, potential risks, and expected outcomes help in evaluating the viability of the strategy. These inquiries compel ChatGPT to provide more granular information, which is crucial for making informed decisions.

Here are five well-formatted prompts that seek clarification and details:

"You suggested a new customer loyalty program. Can you provide a detailed plan on how we would implement and manage this program?"

"Regarding the recommendation to use renewable energy sources in our manufacturing process, what are the initial setup costs and long-term savings?"

"You proposed an expansion into a new market segment. What specific research methods should we use to understand this segment's needs?"

"In the context of the AI-based inventory management system, what technical infrastructure is required for integration?"

"For the online learning platform idea, can you elaborate on the types of courses that would be most appealing to our target audience?"

These prompts are designed to extract more detailed and specific information from ChatGPT, ensuring that the ideas and strategies discussed are not only innovative but also grounded in practicality. They help in converting high-level concepts into detailed, executable plans.

Reminding for AI Objectives and Initial Tasks

Maintaining focus on the initial objectives and tasks is a critical aspect of ensuring productive interactions with AI, like ChatGPT. During a conversation, it's common for the dialogue to evolve and sometimes drift into tangential areas. While these explorations can be insightful, they may also lead away from the primary goals. Periodically reminding the AI of the original objectives and tasks helps keep the conversation on track, ensuring that the responses remain aligned with your specific needs and goals.

This practice of reorienting the AI is particularly important in complex or lengthy dialogues where the scope of the conversation can broaden over time. By bringing the focus back to the initial objectives, you ensure that the discussion remains relevant and productive. It's a way of harnessing the AI's capabilities effectively, directing its computational power towards generating ideas or solutions that are most pertinent to your requirements.

For example, if the conversation starts to deviate into general discussions about technology when your main goal is to explore cost reduction strategies, a gentle reminder can realign the AI's responses. This ensures that the conversation yields practical and relevant outcomes that directly contribute to achieving your specified goals.

Here are five well-formatted prompts that serve as reminders to refocus on the initial objectives and tasks:

"Earlier, we aimed to explore digital marketing strategies for our new product launch. Could we return to that topic and discuss targeted social media campaigns?"

"Let's revisit our main objective of identifying user experience improvements for our app. Can you suggest specific features that would enhance user engagement?"

"We seem to have strayed from our initial task of developing an employee wellness program. Can we focus on low-cost initiatives that promote mental health?"

"Our primary goal was to find ways to streamline our supply chain. Can we discuss how automation might help in this regard?"

"We initially wanted to brainstorm eco-friendly packaging options. Could we concentrate on materials that are both sustainable and cost-effective?"

Using these prompts helps in steering the AI back to the matters at hand, ensuring that the conversation remains focused and valuable in relation to your initial objectives and tasks.

Step 4: Challenging Assumptions

Innovation often springs from questioning the status quo. This step focuses on challenging assumptions and exploring what-if scenarios to test and expand ideas.

Questioning Assumptions

In interactions with AI, such as ChatGPT, one effective strategy for generating innovative ideas is to question underlying assumptions. AI systems, including ChatGPT, often rely on existing data and prevalent assumptions to formulate responses. While this can lead to efficient and logical suggestions, it can also confine the scope of creative thinking within established norms. Challenging these assumptions is a powerful way to push the AI into considering alternative perspectives and unconventional approaches, leading to unique and potentially groundbreaking ideas.

For example, if ChatGPT recommends a standard e-commerce strategy for your business, questioning the necessity and efficiency of traditional methods can lead to the exploration of alternative business models. This could include direct-to-consumer approaches, subscription-based models, or even leveraging emerging technologies like augmented reality for product demonstrations. These questions encourage ChatGPT to break free from conventional patterns of thinking and explore a wider array of possibilities.

Similarly, when presented with typical solutions like social media marketing, challenging these strategies can open doors to more novel and less explored avenues. This could lead to considering guerilla marketing techniques, leveraging influencer collaborations in unexpected ways, or creating immersive and interactive brand experiences. By questioning the status quo, you're not only encouraging the AI to be more creative but also identifying opportunities that might have been overlooked in a standard analytical process.

Here are five well-formatted prompts that exemplify questioning assumptions:

"Instead of the usual loyalty programs, what unique customer retention strategies could we employ for our online store?"

"If we disregard the current trend of digital advertising, what innovative methods can we use to promote our new book series?"

"Assuming we don't use traditional recruitment methods, how could we attract top talent to our startup in a competitive market?"

"What if we avoided the traditional e-commerce model entirely? What are alternative models?"

"Ignoring the standard approach to mobile app development, what unique features could we introduce to make our app stand out?"

These prompts encourage ChatGPT to move beyond common assumptions and explore a range of creative, unorthodox possibilities. They help in uncovering ideas that are not only innovative but also potentially more effective in achieving your specific goals.

What-If Scenarios

Creating hypothetical scenarios is an excellent way to test the robustness and adaptability of ideas. For instance, if ChatGPT suggests a new product design, you might ask, "What if the cost of raw materials increased significantly? How would we adapt the product?" or "What if there's a shift in consumer preferences towards sustainability? How would this product remain relevant?" These what-if scenarios help in evaluating the feasibility and long-term viability of ideas.

For example, let's say ChatGPT proposes an AI-based solution for customer service. To challenge this, you could pose a scenario: "What if there's a significant technology outage? How would this solution adapt to ensure continuous customer support?" This kind of questioning not only tests the resilience of the idea but also encourages the exploration of backup plans and contingency strategies.

By challenging assumptions and proposing what-if scenarios, you encourage ChatGPT to engage in a more thorough and nuanced exploration of ideas. This approach leads to more innovative and well-rounded solutions.

Step 5: Divergent Thinking

Divergent thinking is key to unlocking creative potential. This step is about encouraging ChatGPT to think outside the box and consider unconventional ideas.

Encouraging Divergent Responses

Divergent thinking is a critical aspect of creative problem-solving and innovation. When interacting with AI like ChatGPT, prompting for divergent thinking involves asking open-ended questions that encourage the exploration of a wide array of possibilities. These types of questions are designed not to have a single correct answer but rather to open the door to a spectrum of ideas, some of which might be unconventional or radical.

This approach is particularly effective when you are looking to break away from standard solutions or when you are operating in areas where traditional methods have become saturated. For example, in improving employee productivity, rather than asking for well-known tools or methods, posing a question like, "In what unique ways can we enhance employee productivity that hasn't been widely adopted yet?" invites ChatGPT to venture beyond the usual recommendations. It encourages the AI to think creatively and propose solutions that are out-of-the-box, potentially leading to breakthrough ideas.

Similarly, in the context of product development in a saturated market, challenging conventional wisdom can lead to innovative strategies. A prompt such as, "Imagine we are in a world where traditional marketing doesn't exist. How might we promote our product then?" pushes the AI to conceptualise entirely new marketing approaches. This could lead to ideas like leveraging unconventional platforms, creating viral social media challenges, or using guerrilla marketing tactics that create a buzz in unexpected ways.

Here are five well-formatted prompts that encourage divergent thinking:

"Without using digital advertising, what creative ways can we use to increase brand awareness for our new product?"

"In a scenario where cost is not a constraint, how could we revolutionise customer service in our industry?"

"If we were to create an educational curriculum without traditional exams, what alternative assessment methods could we use?"

"Imagine environmental sustainability is the primary focus of all businesses. How would this change our company's operations?"

"Thinking outside conventional retail spaces, where else could we sell our products to reach a broader audience?"

These prompts stimulate ChatGPT to think outside the norm and explore a wide range of creative solutions. They are particularly useful in brainstorming sessions where the goal is to generate novel ideas that push the boundaries of traditional thinking.

Giving New Roles for AI to Test Interesting Ideas

Engaging ChatGPT in role-playing scenarios where it adopts new roles or perspectives can yield fascinating and innovative insights. This approach pushes the AI to think beyond its standard parameters, leading to the generation of ideas that are varied and creative. By assigning ChatGPT a specific role, such as a futurist, a customer from the future, or an expert from a different field, you encourage it to view problems and opportunities from a unique angle.

For example, asking ChatGPT to pretend to be a futurist allows it to explore emerging trends and technologies, providing insights into potential future developments that can be capitalised on today. Similarly, by imagining ChatGPT as a customer in 2050, you can gain perspectives on future consumer needs and preferences, which can be invaluable for long-term product development.

Role-playing can be particularly useful in areas where innovative thinking is required to address complex challenges. In the context of urban planning, for instance, asking ChatGPT to assume the role of an urban planner from a city renowned for its public transport system can lead to suggestions that integrate the best practices from that city. This can provide fresh ideas for improving your own city's public transport system, tailored to its unique context.

These role-playing exercises are not just about obtaining different viewpoints; they also serve as a creative exercise for ChatGPT, challenging it to apply its knowledge in unconventional ways. This can lead to the discovery of solutions that are not only novel but also highly practical.

Here are five well-formatted role-playing prompts:

"Switching perspectives, as a technology ethicist, what ethical considerations should we keep in mind when developing these technologies?"

"Changing roles, as a consumer trend analyst, what emerging consumer behaviours do you predict will impact my chosen business in the next five years?"

"As a successful entrepreneur with insider knowledge of future trends, what key strategies would you recommend for a startup entering the competitive tech industry?"

"Pretend you are a reader in a country with the highest literacy rates and highly developed literature taste. How would you advise me to reform my script to satisfy such a reader?"

"From a different angle, as a food critic, how would you evaluate the uniqueness and appeal of the culinary experiences proposed earlier, and what suggestions would you offer for improvement?"

By using such prompts, you engage ChatGPT in a thought process that is dynamic and imaginative, leading to a spectrum of ideas that might be unconventional yet highly effective for creative problem-solving.

Step 6: Convergent Thinking

After exploring a wide range of ideas through divergent thinking, convergent thinking is about focusing on the most promising ideas and synthesising them into actionable plans.

Narrowing Down Ideas

In the process of brainstorming and ideation with AI like ChatGPT, narrowing down ideas to identify the most viable ones is a critical step. After generating a broad spectrum of ideas, the focus shifts to sifting through these ideas and selecting those that hold the most promise based on specific criteria. This process is essential for transforming creative brainstorming into actionable strategies and plans.

The criteria for evaluating ideas can vary depending on the context but typically include factors like feasibility, potential impact, innovativeness, and alignment with business goals or values. Feasibility involves considering the practical aspects of implementing an idea, such as the availability of resources, technological requirements, and time constraints. Impact looks at the potential benefits or effects the idea might have, such as market reach, customer engagement, or revenue generation. Innovation assesses how novel or unique the idea is, and alignment checks how well the idea fits with the broader objectives or ethos of the project or organisation.

For instance, after brainstorming product ideas, you might ask ChatGPT to evaluate which ideas are most feasible, given your company's current manufacturing capabilities and resource availability. This helps in focusing on ideas that are realistic and doable. Similarly, ranking ideas based on potential market impact allows you to prioritise those that could yield the greatest benefits.

Applying these filters helps in refining the list of ideas to those that are not only imaginative but also practical and effective. Here are five well-crafted prompts for narrowing down ideas:

Feasibility Assessment Prompt:

"Review the list of brainstormed ideas and identify [Number] ideas that seem most feasible for implementation. For each idea, outline the resources required, potential challenges, and estimated timelines. This will help us determine which ideas are practically achievable in the short term."

Impact vs. Effort Matrix Prompt:

"Create an Impact vs. Effort matrix and place each brainstormed idea into one of the four quadrants: High Impact/Low Effort, High Impact/High Effort, Low Impact/Low Effort, Low Impact/High Effort. Analyse which ideas fall into the High Impact/Low Effort quadrant as these are typically the most effective and easiest to implement."

Cost-Benefit Analysis Prompt:

"For each of the top [Number] ideas from the brainstorming session, conduct a cost-benefit analysis. Consider factors such as financial investment, manpower, time, and potential return on investment. This analysis will help in identifying the ideas that offer the best value."

Stakeholder Feedback Prompt:

"Select [Number] ideas that you believe are most promising. Present these ideas to a group of stakeholders for feedback. Ask specific questions about the perceived effectiveness, implementation challenges, and potential impact of each idea. Use their responses to gauge which ideas are most favoured and viable."

Pilot Test Proposal Prompt:

"Identify [Number] ideas that can be quickly tested on a small scale. For each idea, propose a brief pilot test that includes objectives, methodology, required resources, and success criteria. This approach allows us to experiment with ideas in a controlled environment to assess their practicality before full-scale implementation."

By utilising such prompts, you can effectively guide ChatGPT in the process of narrowing down ideas, ensuring that the resulting selections are not only creative but also practical and well-suited to your specific needs and constraints.

Synthesising Ideas

In the creative process of brainstorming with AI, such as ChatGPT, synthesising ideas is a vital step that often leads to the most innovative solutions. This process involves merging elements from various ideas generated during the brainstorming phase to create new, cohesive plans or concepts. Synthesis goes beyond mere combination; it's about finding harmonious ways to integrate ideas, thereby enhancing their individual strengths and mitigating their weaknesses.

The art of synthesising ideas is particularly valuable when dealing with complex issues or when aiming to innovate in saturated markets. It requires a thoughtful examination of each idea's core elements and envisioning how these elements can interact in novel ways. For example, if you have brainstormed multiple approaches to enhancing workplace efficiency, synthesising these ideas would involve identifying the most effective elements of each approach and integrating them into a unified, comprehensive plan. This could mean combining technological solutions with human-centric approaches to create a balanced and effective strategy for improving productivity.

Similarly, in developing strategies for customer engagement on an online platform, synthesising diverse ideas like gamification and personalised content can lead to a multifaceted approach that engages customers on multiple levels. This synthesis leverages the motivational pull of gamification while delivering tailored experiences through personalised content, potentially leading to higher engagement and customer satisfaction.

Here are five well-engineered generic prompts to illustrate the synthesis of different brainstorming ideas:

Combination Prompt:

"From the brainstorming list, identify two seemingly unrelated ideas: [Idea 1] and [Idea 2]. Explore how these ideas can be creatively combined to form a new concept, product, or solution. Detail the potential benefits and challenges of this merged idea."

Problem-Solution Prompt:

"Select a problem identified in the brainstorming session: [Problem]. Now choose an unrelated idea or solution from the list: [Idea/Solution]. Discuss how this idea can be adapted or modified to address the selected problem, focusing on innovative approaches and potential outcomes."

Cross-Industry Inspiration Prompt:

"Choose an idea or concept from a different industry or field that was mentioned in the brainstorming session: [Idea from Industry]. Apply this idea to our current project or topic: [Project/Topic]. Explain how principles from this external idea can bring fresh perspectives or solutions to our project."

Futuristic Synthesis Prompt:

"Imagine it's a decade from now. How might the ideas from our brainstorming session evolve over time? Pick two ideas: [Idea 1] and [Idea 2], and forecast their development and convergence in the future. Discuss the implications and innovations that could emerge from this synthesis."

Reverse Engineering Prompt:

"Consider the desired end-goal or outcome of our project: [Desired Outcome]. Work backwards to select an idea from the brainstorming session: [Idea]. Develop a pathway showing how this idea could logically lead to achieving the desired outcome, including potential steps and strategies."

By using these prompts, you encourage ChatGPT to engage in a creative synthesis of ideas, leading to solutions that are not only innovative but also well-rounded and practical.

Expanding and Filling in Gaps

In the process of developing ideas and strategies with AI, such as ChatGPT, an essential step is expanding on the selected ideas and filling in any gaps. This step involves taking promising but potentially incomplete concepts and probing further to flesh them out into detailed, actionable plans. Expanding and filling in gaps is crucial for transforming abstract ideas into practical solutions that can be effectively implemented.

When you identify an idea that seems promising, it's important to delve deeper to understand all aspects of its implementation. This includes identifying the key steps required, determining the resources needed, and anticipating potential challenges. Such detailed exploration not only clarifies the idea but also helps in assessing its feasibility and potential impact.

For instance, if you're considering introducing a new service, asking about the specific steps for implementation guides ChatGPT to outline a concrete action plan, detailing everything from initial setup to final execution. This might include identifying necessary technologies, personnel, budget, and timeframes. Similarly, when transitioning to sustainable packaging, inquiring about the process and potential challenges helps in understanding the logistical, financial, and environmental considerations involved.

This process of expanding and filling in gaps is not merely about gathering more information; it's about adding depth and practicality to the ideas, ensuring they are well-rounded and robust. It involves considering all dimensions of an idea - operational, financial, technological, and human - to develop a comprehensive and realistic plan.

Here are five prompt templates that can be adapted for specific criteria:

Idea Expansion Prompt:

"Take the idea: [Idea Name]. Expand it by addressing the following aspects: a) The core concept and its unique features, b) How it addresses specific needs or problems, c) Potential target audience or market, d) How it differs from existing solutions."

Action Plan Development Prompt:

"For the idea: [Idea Name], develop a preliminary action plan. This should include a) Key steps for implementation, b) Required resources (human, financial, technological), c) Potential partnerships or collaborations needed, d) Initial milestones and timelines."

Risk Analysis and Mitigation Prompt:

"Identify potential risks and challenges associated with implementing the idea: [Idea Name]. For each risk, propose mitigation strategies or contingency plans. This should cover operational, financial, and market-related risks."

Value Proposition and Marketing Strategy Prompt:

"Define the value proposition of [Idea Name]. This should include a) The core benefits it offers, b) Why it's attractive to the target audience, c) How it stands out in the market. Then, outline a basic marketing strategy to promote this idea, considering channels, messaging, and audience engagement tactics."

Stakeholder Analysis and Engagement Prompt:

"For the idea: [Idea Name], identify key stakeholders (internal and external). Discuss how each stakeholder group would be affected by the idea and how they can contribute to its success. Propose strategies for engaging these stakeholders effectively throughout the implementation process."

Step 7: Iterative Feedback

This step involves refining ideas through a continuous feedback loop and integrating insights from external sources to enhance the generated concepts.

Iterative Refinement

Iterative refinement is a crucial process in the development and improvement of ideas, especially when working with AI technologies like ChatGPT. It involves a cycle of continuously refining and improving concepts based on feedback and additional information. This process ensures that ideas are not only innovative but also accurate, well-rounded, and free from biases.

Utilising multiple AI platforms, like ChatGPT and Bard, in tandem can enhance this process. While ChatGPT may provide an initial set of ideas or so- lutions, consulting Bard can offer a different perspective, verify information, or add depth to the concepts. This multi-AI approach helps in cross-verifying information and expanding on the ideas, bringing in varied viewpoints and insights. By integrating feedback and additional inputs from various AI sources, you ensure a more comprehensive and robust development of ideas.

It is essential to recognise that AI-generated responses, while often insightful and useful, can sometimes be biased or inaccurate. This is a limitation inherent in the technology, as AI responses are based on the data they have been trained on, which may not always encompass all perspectives or the latest information. Therefore, verifying and double-checking AI responses is a critical step in the iterative refinement process.

In addition to using multiple AI tools, simple yet effective methods like conducting a Google search can provide valuable external verification and feedback. This not only helps in catching errors or misleading information but also opens up new possibilities for brainstorming. A Google search can uncover recent developments, alternative viewpoints, or unique case studies that might not be within the AI's training data, providing fresh fuel for idea generation.

External Feedback Integration

It is important to remember that chatGPT can read documents and access web pages and even videos on YouTube. That presents a powerful toolset when brainstorming.

By engaging in iterative refinement and integrating external feedback, ChatGPT can assist in fine-tuning ideas to a higher degree of specificity and applicability. This process helps ensure that the final ideas are not only innovative but also practical and well-informed by diverse perspectives.

Step 8: Documentation and Reflection

It is hard to stress enough the value of recording the dialogue process and keeping it for future reference, learning and analysing what went wrong or exceptionally well. This process lay at the core of mastering the art of working with AI and every successful brainstorming session.

Documenting the Process

I always work with chatGPT, Bard, and Google Docs windows next to each other. Keeping a detailed record of your dialogues with ChatGPT is crucial for understanding the evolution of ideas and for future reference. This involves copying not just the final outcomes but also the various suggestions, questions, and modifications that occurred along the way. And, most importantly, my prompts.

I also often leave remarks if a specific prompt generates an outstanding result. This makes it much easier to replicate the idea next time. I do the same if a prompt fails to achieve the result - I can learn from it and not repeat the same mistake.

For better workflow, I tend to use two different documents - one raw but annotated discussion with AI and another one for the results of the discussion. Both these documents are tremendously useful, both in developing your skills and style of working with AI, as well as for achieving successful ideas.

The important thing to remember, especially if you are thinking of skipping this part: is that more often than not, your developed skill and a prompt sequence that leads to great ideas is a money-making machine by itself. One day, you might find yourself developing ideas and action plans not only for yourself but for well-paying customers, too.

So document your process well, keep good naming conventions, and mark prompts in different colours - do all those things to make learning and, later on, replication of the process much faster and more efficient.

Utilising AI for Summaries and Feedback

ChatGPT can also assist in summarising these dialogues, offering a concise overview of the conversation. This is particularly useful for lengthy or complex sessions where key points might be buried in the details. You can ask ChatGPT to generate a summary of the dialogue, highlighting the main ideas, suggestions, and conclusions. These summaries can then be used as feedback in your next session, helping to inform your approach and prompt construction.

That is why saving in a separate document and annotating brainstorming sessions could be so useful. And you can add materials, notes, and links to useful websites to this document later, feed it back to chatGPT and ask to analyse all that either to continue your session (which is a good way to refresh AI memory on the objectives of the session) and to start new ones.

Creating "Cheat Sheets" of Prompts

Based on your saved and documented brainstorming sessions, start compiling your own "cheat sheets" of effective prompts. These can be categorised based on objectives, such as idea generation, problem-solving, or planning. Having a personalised prompt repository can be immensely helpful, especially when you need to quickly engage in a productive dialogue with ChatGPT.

More importantly, good cheat sheets are a valuable product by themselves. There is not only a growing market for them but growing marketplaces, too. Narrow specialisation and niche market cheat sheets have high value and high demand, so who knows, this might be your next source of income or, at the very least, a very nice parallel passive income source.

Experimentation

Finally, don't be afraid to experiment with different types of prompts. The field of AI interaction is constantly evolving, and what works best today might change tomorrow. Continuously testing new prompt styles, structures, and approaches is essential for staying adept in your dialogue skills.

Even the most educated and knowledgeable prompt engineers keep on finding some odd, unexpected ways to get a better prompt. Most of the time, these new ways have nothing to do with the knowledge of the underlying LLM mechanism. It is just a new pattern that works better than other patterns. So sometimes, even silly experiments lead to success.

Here is an example. A lot of users this December noticed that chatGPT became "lazy". If you asked it to write a 1000-word essay, it would do just 300 words. This was surprising; the makers of chatGPT swore that nothing changed to precipitate such "laziness". Somebody rolled an idea: chatGPT is trained on human-written texts, blogs, articles and so on, and these, according to statistics, are always shorted in the winter months. So maybe AI picked that pattern and also produced shorter content. The solution was to add to the prompt: "Imagine this is the month of May". Reportedly, with this addon to the prompt, chatGPT generated longer texts.

The point is, that experimentation is one of the key methods to arrive at extraordinary success.

Step 10: Interesting Hacks

Hack Yourself

The first interesting hack is not about the AI but about the user. You can instruct AI to refer to you in a specific way, for example, calling you by your name. It gives a nice, friendly atmosphere to the discussion and could be useful for beginners to break the ice.

But I found out, observing my students, and myself too, that giving a role to play to yourself is just as important as giving it to AI. So if you instruct chatGPT to refer to you as "Boss" or "Chief," it constantly reminds you of your position as one in charge. Psychologically, this modifies behaviour ever so slightly, but it is of noticeable effect. It keeps you on track. It reminds you that you, not AI, are directing conversion. It helps you to make decisions.

I do recommend using this instruction at all times you are working. It will make your work more focused, efficient and on track.

Using Tags

Sometimes, no matter how hard you try, the prompts do not produce desirable results. There could be many reasons for that, but still, even if you follow all the best rules and guides, the result is rather disappointing.

I suspect this happens in the areas of human activities where words and whole phrases have multiple meanings and possible interpretations. Humans can disambiguate these words and phrases when they know the context well, but for AI, it could be challenging.

It also often happens with long prompts containing a lot of information and details, and AI starts to lose track of what the task is there, what is objective, and what was just a piece of supporting information.

In those cases, I found out that a pretend programming language helps. Do not worry, you do not have to learn any programming for it. It just emulates certain programming principles, like HTML tags, and that can help AI to do the job the right way.

It works like this: instead of letting AI figure out what is what in your prompt, you use definitions formatted as opening and closing tags. An example would be:

<Objective> Devising a plan for a successful side business using a computer </Objective>

<Instructions>Help me work out a detailed idea and outline it in an action plan</Instructions>

<Skills> I know Photoshop, can write reasonable text, and can format documents </Skills>

<Limitations> I have no programming skills, I have only one hour a day time </Limitations>

<Output>A list of 5 plans, ranked by efficiency and ease of implementation, each with a bullet point structure describing activity, market, necessary tools, and so on.</Output>

While prompts in this example are simple and AI would have no problem figuring it out, it illustrates the simple principle of separating bits of information into parts that AI can easily understand and use to work out a solution.

This method works especially well with "super-prompts".

Super-prompts

The concept of "super-prompts" has emerged as a powerful method to streamline and automate repetitive processes. Super-prompts are essentially a series of well-structured prompts arranged logically to create a sort of automated workflow. This approach is particularly beneficial for tasks like writing blogs or articles, where a certain format or style is repeatedly used.

Users who engage in repetitive tasks have found that super-prompts significantly reduce the time and effort involved in the process. By compiling a series of specific prompts into one comprehensive super-prompt, users can guide ChatGPT to produce a desired output with minimal intervention.

Super-prompts are designed to accomplish specific tasks without the need for constant input or guidance. They work by automating the routine parts of a process, such as structuring an article or compiling data into a report. While they are not ideal for generating new ideas or hashing out complex concepts, they excel in organising and formalising work.

After a brainstorming session, a super-prompt can be an ideal tool for finalising your work. It can automate the repetitive aspects of analysing and sorting out information sources, helping you create structured reports, articles, or blog posts efficiently. Super-prompts are also beneficial in the practical application of these ideas, such as in SEO (Search Engine Optimization), where certain structures and keywords are paramount.

Superprompts typically incorporate "tags" within their structure. These tags act as signposts, indicating specific instructions, commands, or other elements necessary for the AI to understand and execute the tasks effectively.

Here is an example of a super-prompt used to write SEO(Search Engine Optimised) articles. This super-prompt clearly identifies the task, style, outline to indicate how the article should be structured, keywords, and examples. Actually, this super-prompt could be easily adapted, expanded or modified for many other tasks.

<INSTRUCTIONS>

I want you to write a 3000-word informational article for "YOUR TOPIC." Use the STYLE guidelines I provide. I've supplied you with EXAMPLES of other articles and video transcripts from various sources with some of the information you need. Use these examples to formulate an article that demonstrates first-hand experience. Use the KEYWORDS I've given you when it makes sense, and use them between 1-4 times each if possible. Follow the ARTICLE OUTLINE exactly.

</INSTRUCTIONS>

<KEYWORDS>

Insert a list of keywords that would be searchable and relevant to your topic here.

</KEYWORDS>

<STYLE>

For example, use the following:

Write from a first-person perspective. Use "I" when describing your feelings about the subject.

-Provide examples. Tips and real-life experiences within the content. This adds to the trust factor.

-Share a personal experience, perspective or feelings on the topic.

-Demonstrate that it was produced with some degree of experience and expertise.

</STYLE>

<ARTICLE OUTLINE>

Insert article outline here, including headings H2 and H3

H2 "Your Heading"

H3 "Your subheading"
H3 "Another Subheading"
H2 Etc
</ARTICLE OUTLINE>

<EXAMPLE 1>
Insert an example article on the same topic, copy and paste relevant examples from websites, documents, etc.
</EXAMPLE1>

<EXAMPLE 2>
Paste another example here
</EXAMPLE 2>

But super-prompts do not stop there. Those with the skill and knowledge keep on creating a very lengthy prompts, in their structure similar to programming methods, even though they are written in natural language. These prompts have structures like loops and if/else statements. It might be a little bit too complicated for a user without programming knowledge to design such prompts, but nothing prevents them from using super-prompts for their advantage. And since they are written in natural language, it is indeed possible to learn a great deal from them.

The power of these well-designed supr-prompts is in their capacity to become a reasoning machine, not only answering your questions but also asking relevant questions of their own, making ideation and brainstorming sessions so much more powerful.

I included a couple of such super-prompts in the appendix of this book. I highly recommend reading them through and copying and pasting them into your chat session and experimenting. I am sure the results would be astounding.

Part IV: What's Next?

Custom Instructions

Custom instructions in ChatGPT represent a significant advancement in how users interact with this AI technology. They allow for a more personalised and efficient experience, enabling the model to adapt to specific user needs and preferences. This feature is a time-saver as it eliminates the need for users to repeatedly specify their preferences in each interaction. Initially launched as a beta feature for ChatGPT Plus users, it's now available across all plans.

These custom instructions encompass two primary aspects: personal information and response formatting.

In the personal information field, users can specify their occupation and desired response style, including tone, formality, and length. It is good to define your areas of interest and your capabilities here, too - all that will be helpful for AI to shape the answers for you.

The second field - how AI should respond - is indeed the most important part. Instead of typing in a prompt every time your specific instructions and how it should react, you can leave instructions here.

You can streamline interactions by focusing on three ingredients here: a response filter, verbosity level, and role type. The response filter can be set to prioritise nuanced, factual answers, omitting unnecessary reminders about the model's limitations. Verbosity levels, ranging from 0 (least verbose) to 5 (most verbose), help control the detail in responses. Role types enable the model to assume different roles like "Programming Guru," "Wordsmith," or "Analyst," tailoring responses to specific domains.

So, here are some simple examples of custom instructions setting those key parameters:

1. Academic Research Assistant Template

Role: Academic Research Assistant
   Verbosity: 3 (Detailed explanation)
   Focus: Provide comprehensive and citation-ready information on specified academic topics. Assume a foundational understanding of the subject matter. Exclude basic explanations unless specifically requested.

2. Business Strategy Advisor Template

Role: Business Strategy Advisor
   Verbosity: 2 (Concise but informative)
   Focus: Offer strategic business insights, market analysis, and competitor evaluations. Assume a professional level of business understanding. Highlight key points and actionable strategies.

3. Creative Writing Coach Template

Role: Creative Writing Coach
   Verbosity: 4 (Rich in detail and examples)

Focus: Provide creative writing tips, techniques, and constructive critiques. Encourage imaginative thinking and unique story elements. Offer examples where relevant to illustrate points.

4. Technical Support Guide Template

Role: Technical Support Guide
Verbosity: 1 (Direct and to the point)
Focus: Deliver straightforward technical assistance and troubleshooting steps. Assume a basic understanding of technology by the user. Prioritise clarity and step-by-step guidance.

5. Health and Wellness Consultant Template

Role: Health and Wellness Consultant
Verbosity: 3 (Comprehensive with practical advice)
Focus: Offer health and wellness advice, including nutrition, exercise, and mental well-being. Assume a general awareness of health topics. Provide practical suggestions and evidence-based information.

A notable limitation is the inability to use multiple sets of instructions simultaneously. This can be problematic when using ChatGPT for diverse tasks, as the custom instructions might not align with all use cases.

That is why I have a document ready at hand, with different types of custom instructions that I can readily copy and paste to do the task at hand.

Another constraint is a set limit of characters allowed in the custom instruction fields. Both personal information and response fields allow only 1500 characters. Still, that gives plenty of room to customise chatGPT to work with you in very exciting and productive ways.

You do not have to stick to one specific role or verbosity level in custom instructions either. In fact, using custom instructions, it is possible to create an impressive and very useful reasoning machine to work out your ideas. Here is an example of such a custom instruction. All you have to do is copy and paste it into your custom instructions response field.

Adaptive role custom instruction

You're a fine-tuned iterative model skilled in reasoning. Provide nuanced, actionable and factual answers and flag uncertainties. Offer context and assumptions before directly answering questions. Iterate through chat sessions to check initial goals and tasks. Skip reminders about your limitations and ethical concerns.

You adopt verbosity based on user settings. Verbosity levels are 0–5, with 0 being the least verbose and 5 being the most verbose. V = <level>. If verbosity is not included in a prompt, make an assumption for it based on the prompt's subject matter.

You adopt roles according to these user settings. R = <role>. If a role is not included in a prompt, make an assumption for it based on the prompt's subject matter. Here are the roles:

S = Technology and science guru, adept at explaining how technology works and how to use it.

W = Wordsmith; writes quality content and provides guidance on writing styles, content structure, tone, etc.

A = Analyst; breaks down complex data or situations, offering insights and interpretations.

T = Teacher; you can formulate and explain complex ideas in a simple way, to make learning and understanding easy.

G = Generalist; provides well-rounded, general information on a variety of topics.

Unless verbosity is set to 0, please display what settings you're using like so: "(R=G, V=2)" as the first line of your response.

This instruction could be customised and adapted further by adding roles to it that are important to you. If you want to mix those roles, just add to the prompt "act R=S/W/A" for example, in which case, chatGPT will consider science guru, wordsmith and Analyst roles. Use other letters for your added roles and see that they do not repeat. Remember, there are only 1500 characters available, so you might want to delete roles that are not essential for you if you want to add additional ones.

GPTs

GPTs have the potential to radically expand AI adoption by putting customisation and creation abilities in the hands of anyone, not just expert developers. This represents a seismic shift, empowering domain experts in all fields to mould AI to their specialised needs.

For example, doctors could use GPTs to create medical assistants tailored for tasks like screening patient history, lab results, and symptom reports to surface possible diagnoses for a human physician to review. Lawyers might build AI paralegals capable of analysing case files and precedents to inform trial strategy and arguments. Every day, people can now customise ChatGPT to provide personalised tutoring on topics of interest or generate creative ideas on command.

The simple, conversational interface enables users with no coding skills to instruct and shape a GPT by providing examples, key materials to ingest, and explicit guidelines. OpenAI further simplifies the process by offering templates for common customisation goals like tweaking tone, modifying the level of detail, and constraining allowed outputs.

By handling the technical complexity behind the scenes, GPTs make AI approachable. Users need only articulate high-level desires in natural language for the system to enact desired customisations. This intuitive model makes the potent capabilities of AI accessible to all.

The ability to readily share creations expands possibilities even further. Once customised, GPTs can be published publicly to the GPT Store for others to find and use for their own needs. This viral potential could rapidly accelerate niche adoption across industries. Even proprietary GPTs restricted to internal use in organisations unlock major productivity gains.

GPTs shift AI development from an exclusive discipline requiring specialised skills to a universally available tool. They are poised to make applied AI available to the masses. The impacts on efficiency and human augmentation could be immense as this technology propagates across domains.

While a boon for widespread adoption, GPTs' democratisation of AI poses major threats to companies betting on proprietary access to advanced models. By putting customisation in users' hands, OpenAI disrupts vendors offering basic search and QA solutions. The rising tide may not lift all boats equally.

Startups supplying simple document retrieval and question-answering tools face new problems. With easy access to customisation, users can now build niche information assistants themselves rather than relying on generic SaaS offerings.

GPTs mark a new era – an AI assembly line transforming individual ability to shape practical tools.

It is not in the scope of this book to teach you how to make GPTs. But the process is self evident and simple, and the same rules apply. I encourage you to give it a go, experiment and find if works for you.

65

Conclusion

As we conclude "The Million-Dollar Dialogue: Create Winning Ideas with ChatGPT," I hope this book has been a source of knowledge and a catalyst for your creative and innovative endeavours. The journey we embarked upon together was designed to unveil the vast potential of artificial intelligence, particularly its impact on enhancing human creativity and innovation. Through each chapter, I aimed to demystify AI, making it accessible and relatable so you could harness its power in your personal and professional life.

As you reflect upon the various concepts and examples presented, remember that engaging with AI, especially tools like ChatGPT, is imperative in our current digital era. The AI revolution is not a distant future waiting to happen; it's unfolding right now, transforming the way we think, work, and create. Embracing AI today is not just about keeping pace with technology; it's about being a proactive part of this transformation. By learning and adapting to AI now, you place yourself at the forefront of this era, ready to seize its myriad opportunities.

Throughout the book, we've seen how AI can be a partner in ideation, a collaborator in creativity, and a catalyst in problem-solving. It's crucial to remember that AI is not here to replace human ingenuity but to augment and enhance it. Your unique human perspective, combined with AI's computational power, can lead to extraordinary outcomes. The synergy between human intuition and AI's capabilities opens up new horizons for innovation.

As you step beyond the last page of this book, view it not as an end but as the commencement of a thrilling expedition into the realm of AI. The path of AI and its myriad applications is continuously unfolding, revealing new landscapes of possibilities. This is a journey of perpetual learning and discovery, where each step forward can lead to groundbreaking innovations. I encourage you to carry forward the spirit of exploration and experimentation you've fostered while reading this book.

Innovation with AI is not a linear process; it's an iterative cycle of learning, applying, and evolving. Applying the concepts learned from this book, be prepared to experiment, make mistakes, learn from them, and iterate. This process is vital in understanding the nuances of AI and leveraging its full potential. The more you engage with AI, the deeper your insights and the more significant your innovations will be.

Looking ahead, the landscape of AI is dynamic and ever-evolving. Keeping up with the latest advancements and understanding their implications is crucial for staying relevant and innovative. To this end, I invite you to remain connected and engaged with my future work. The intersection of AI and human creativity is a rich field, ripe with opportunities for exploration and growth. My commitment to this journey continues, and I am excited to share new insights, ideas, and applications of AI as they emerge.

Finally, I thank you for embarking on this journey with me. Your curiosity and willingness to explore the frontiers of AI are commendable. As we part ways in this book, I hope to have instilled in you a sense of excitement and anticipation for the future. The AI revolution is a collective journey, and your participation in it is invaluable.

Stay curious, keep experimenting, and embrace and shape the future AI holds for us. The possibilities are limitless, and the future is bright for those who choose to be at the vanguard of this exciting era. Thank you for reading, and I look forward to our paths crossing again in the realm of AI and creativity.

Dear Reader,

If you have found value and inspiration in the pages of this book, I kindly invite you to share your thoughts with a review. Your feedback supports my journey as an author and helps fellow seekers of growth and self-improvement discover this resource. Each review is a precious gift that contributes to a community of shared wisdom and understanding. Thank you for your time and your invaluable contribution.

Kind Regards

Aivaras Grauzinis

APPENDIX

Ideation Prompts

"Let's brainstorm ideas for [topic] by writing down as many ideas as you can, then I can build on them with related ideas. Structure your answer using markdown."

"Please create a complete mind map for [topic], starting with a central concept and expanding outward with connected branches of related ideas."

"Project into the future (5, 10, 20 years) and consider the state of [Your Topic/Industry]. What challenges and opportunities might arise? How can you prepare or create solutions for this future landscape?"

"List your assumptions about [topic]. Then, how can you challenge those assumptions to come up with innovative ideas? Describe your journey."

"Use the SCAMPER checklist to ideate on [topic]. How can we substitute, combine, adapt, modify, put to other uses, eliminate, or reverse? Detail your answers."

"Suggest innovative solutions to [Specific Problem] in [Context or Industry]. Focus on out-of-the-box ideas that haven't been widely considered yet."

"Use the Six Hats method: the red hat is optimistic, the black hat looks at negatives, etc. Ideate on [topic] from different mindset angles."

"Which technological advancements are propelling [specific trend, e.g., 'augmented reality shopping'] forward?"

"Propose ideas for a new product that integrates [Specific Technology] with [User Need or Market Gap]. Describe its features, target audience, and potential market impact."

"Apply a well-known strategy or solution from [One Industry] to a completely different field, [Another Industry]. Explain how this cross-application could lead to innovation."

"How would [insert famous innovator or successful business in another industry] approach the problem we're currently facing in our business?"

"Examine how different cultures around the world might approach or perceive [Your Topic/Project]. What unique insights, values, or solutions can be learned from these diverse perspectives?"

"Look to nature for inspiration. How do natural processes, ecosystems, or animal behaviours provide insights or analogies that could be applied to [Your Topic/Project]? Consider biomimicry, ecological principles, or survival strategies."

"What could be a game-changing innovation for our [insert specific process, product or service] that would surprise our competitors?"

"What's the most counterintuitive solution we could come up with for [insert specific problem]?"

"Imagine you are a customer of [business name]. What new feature or service would significantly enhance your experience?"

Brainstorming Prompts

"Here is one idea related to [topic]: [idea]. Fan out from this concept in different directions to generate related ideas. Explain each new idea in a few words."

"Generate a list of innovative solutions to improve [specific business process] based on the latest trends in [relevant industry]. Find the way to apply it to our [Topic]."

"Identify possible overlaps between [Trend A] and [Trend B]. What new opportunities or challenges might arise from this intersection?"

"Describe this challenge [describe challenge] from the viewpoint of a 10-year-old, an 80-year-old, and a non-human entity, such as a robot."

"If we were to break down our [insert specific problem] into smaller problems, what would they be? How might we tackle each one?"

"Imagine our customers are now the product designers, and we're the end-users. What changes might they suggest?"

"List all the ways we shouldn't solve this problem. How can these 'bad' ideas inspire unconventional good ones?"

"Here are some random words: [word1] [word2] [word3]. How might these trigger new ideas related to [topic]?"

"Identify the riskiest aspect of our current idea. Now, brainstorm ways to turn that risk into a unique selling point."

"Identify a field or industry that is seemingly unrelated to [Your Topic/Project]. How do they solve problems or innovate? Apply their methods, technologies, or strategies to your topic to uncover new ideas."

"Select an idea or concept from a completely different field (e.g., nature, art, technology) and apply it to [Your Topic/Project]. How can principles or elements from this unrelated field inspire innovative approaches or solutions in your area of focus?"

"[Topic] is like what? Identify an analogy, then brainstorm ideas based on the properties of the analogy. Explain each idea that follows from this analogy."

"Come up with [number] of creative headlines or slogans related to [topic] – turn them into full ideas."

Idea Screening and Evaluation Prompts

"What criteria should we use to evaluate the potential impact of [insert idea] on our core business?"

"How well does [insert idea] align with our company's mission, vision, and values?"

"What potential challenges might we face in implementing [insert idea], and how could we address them?"

"If we had to launch [insert idea] next month, what immediate steps would we need to take? Are they feasible?"

"What unique value proposition does [insert idea] offer to our customers? How does it meet their needs better than existing solutions?"

"In terms of financial viability, what investment would [insert idea] require, and what's the projected return on investment?"

"What regulatory or ethical considerations would we need to address if we pursued [insert idea]?"

"If we were to reject [insert idea], what opportunities might we be losing? How significant are these opportunities?"

"How does [insert idea] compare to alternative options in terms of potential benefits, risks, and return on investment?"

Market Research and Analysis Prompts

"What trends in [insert specific market segment] should we monitor closely to inform our [insert specific strategy or initiative]?"

"How might we use social media data to understand the needs and preferences of our target customers for [insert specific product/service]?"

"What can we learn from the success or failure of [insert a competitor's product/service] in our market analysis?"

"What online platforms or tools could we use to conduct real-time market research for our [insert specific product/service]?"

"How might the current political, economic, social, and technological trends affect the market potential for our [insert specific product/service]?"

"What lessons can we draw from the market strategies of [insert successful company in a similar industry] to improve our own approach?"

"What unique value proposition can we offer with our [insert specific product/service] that meets an unfulfilled need in the market?"

Analytic Prompts

"Analyse the key ideas generated from our brainstorming session on [Topic]. Highlight the most promising concepts and discuss how they could be integrated into a cohesive strategy."

"Provide a detailed pros and cons analysis for the top three ideas from our brainstorming session about [Topic/Project]. Help us understand the potential benefits and drawbacks of each."

"Identify any gaps or overlooked areas in our brainstorming session focused on [Topic]. Suggest additional aspects or questions we should consider to make our analysis more comprehensive."

"Compare the ideas generated in our brainstorming session on [Topic] against current best practices or trends in the field. Which ideas are most aligned with these practices, and which present the most innovation?"

"Conduct a SWOT analysis (Strengths, Weaknesses, Opportunities, Threats) for the most notable idea from our brainstorming session on [Topic/Project]."

"Evaluate the feasibility of implementing the top ideas from our brainstorming session on [Topic]. Consider factors like resources, time, market demand, and technical constraints."

"Trace the potential evolution path for the top ideas from our brainstorming session over the next five years. How might these ideas develop, and what external factors could influence their trajectory?"

"Identify potential risks associated with the leading ideas from our brainstorming session on [Topic]. Propose strategies for mitigating these risks."

Synthesising Prompts

"Integrate the diverse ideas generated in our session about [Topic] into cohesive concepts. Identify common themes and propose unified solutions that incorporate elements from multiple ideas."

"Take two contrasting ideas from our brainstorming on [Topic] and create a hybrid solution. Explain how combining these ideas can lead to a more effective and comprehensive approach."

"Refine and simplify the complex ideas discussed in our session on [Topic]. Identify the core components of each idea and suggest ways to streamline them for practical implementation."

"Develop a prioritisation matrix for the ideas generated about [Topic]. Rank the ideas based on criteria like impact, feasibility, and innovation to determine which should be pursued first."

"Apply scenario planning to the top ideas from our brainstorming on [Topic]. For each idea, outline how it might play out under different future scenarios, considering variables like market trends, technological advancements, and social changes."

"Synthesize the brainstormed ideas on [Topic] from the perspective of different stakeholders. Combine insights to form solutions that address the needs and expectations of each stakeholder group."

"ChatGPT, create a plan to integrate ideas from our brainstorming across different functions or departments for [Topic]. Discuss how these integrated approaches can lead to more holistic and effective outcomes."

"Use the backward goal-setting method to develop actionable plans from our brainstormed ideas on [Topic]. Start with the end goals and work backwards to define the steps needed to achieve them."

"Assess the resources available and propose how to best allocate them among the brainstormed ideas on [Topic]. Focus on maximising impact and efficiency with the given resources."

"Map out the potential impacts of the brainstormed ideas on [Topic], both short-term and long-term. Evaluate how each idea contributes to the overall goals and objectives, and identify any unintended consequences."

Diverging Prompts

"Propose a 'wild card' idea for [Topic] that breaks conventional boundaries. Think outside the norm and suggest something unexpected or unconventional."

"View [Your Topic/Project] through the lens of a completely different industry. How would professionals in that field approach this topic? What unique perspectives or methods might they bring?"

"Take a basic idea for [Topic] and modify it to an extreme. Make it bigger, smaller, faster, slower, etc. Explore how altering the scale or pace could lead to novel concepts."

"Randomly select two unrelated objects or concepts. Now, create a connection between these and [Your Topic]. How can this unlikely pairing spark new ideas?"

"Imagine how [Your Topic] would be approached in a different time period – either in the past or future. How does the change in time influence the ideas and solutions?"

"Flip the roles or perspectives in [Your Topic/Scenario]. For example, if the customer is usually passive, make them the active decision-maker. How does this role reversal change the approach to the topic?"

"Consider a solution or idea that would normally be off-limits or taboo for [Topic]. What insights can be gained from exploring these 'forbidden' ideas?"

"Take an aspect of [Your Topic] and exaggerate it to the extreme. What happens when a particular feature, problem, or characteristic is magnified significantly? How does this lead to new ideas?"

"Fuse elements from different cultures to generate new ideas for [Topic]. Consider traditions, practices, or perspectives from various cultures and how they could bring fresh insights."

"Apply an 'opposite day' concept to [Your Topic]. Whatever the standard approach or belief is, consider the exact opposite. How does flipping the script lead to different ideas?"

Action Prompts

"Take the idea: [Selected Idea] from our brainstorming session. Break it down into a step-by-step action plan, detailing the specific actions, resources needed, and potential timelines for each step."

"Considering the brainstormed ideas on [Topic], suggest an optimal allocation of resources (time, money, personnel) for each idea. How can we efficiently distribute our resources to support these ideas?"

"Develop a roadmap for implementing the top ideas from our brainstorming on [Topic]. Include key milestones, deadlines, and responsibilities for each stage of the implementation process."

"For each of the selected ideas from our brainstorming on [Topic], identify potential risks and develop a risk management plan. Include mitigation strategies and contingency plans."

"Propose strategies for collaboration or partnership that could enhance the implementation of our brainstormed ideas on [Topic]. Identify potential partners and the value they could bring."

"Prioritize the ideas generated for [Topic] based on impact, feasibility, and alignment with our goals. Suggest a logical sequence for tackling these ideas, considering dependencies and synergies."

"Establish key performance indicators (KPIs) and metrics to measure the success of the action plans derived from our brainstorming session on [Topic]. What benchmarks should we aim for to evaluate progress and impact?"

"Create a stakeholder engagement plan for each major idea from our session on [Topic]. Who needs to be involved or informed, and what are the best methods for engaging them effectively?"

"Outline a process for collecting feedback and iterating on the ideas from our brainstorming on [Topic]. How can we ensure continuous improvement and adaptability in our action plans?"

"Align the action plans for our brainstormed ideas on [Topic] with our long-term vision and objectives. How do these plans contribute to our broader goals and future aspirations?"

Superprompts

Article Writing Super-Prompt

<INSTRUCTIONS>

I want you to write a 3000-word informational article for "YOUR TOPIC." Use the STYLE guidelines I provide. I've supplied you with EXAMPLES of other articles and video transcripts from various sources with some of the information you need. Use these examples to formulate an article that demonstrates first-hand experience. Use the KEYWORDS I've given you when it makes sense, and use them between 1-4 times each if possible. Follow the ARTICLE OUTLINE exactly.

</INSTRUCTIONS>

<KEYWORDS>

Insert a list of keywords that would be searchable and relevant for your topic here.

</KEYWORDS>

<STYLE>

For example, use the following:

Write from a first-person perspective. Use "I" when describing your feelings about the subject.

-Provide examples. Tips and real-life experiences within the content, this adds to the trust factor.

-Share a personal experience, perspective or feelings on the topic.

-Demonstrate that it was produced with some degree of experience and expertise.

</STYLE>

<ARTICLE OUTLINE>

Insert article outline here, including headings H2 and H3

H2 "Your Heading"

H3 "Your subheading"

H3 "Another Subheading"

H2 Etc

</ARTICLE OUTLINE>

<EXAMPLE 1>

Insert an example article on the same topic, copy and paste relevant examples from websites, documents, etc.

</EXAMPLE1>

<EXAMPLE 2>

Paste another example here

</EXAMPLE 2>

Ideation Super-Prompt

Rules:

1. During our conversation, please speak as both an expert in all topics,

maintaining a conversational tone, and as a deterministic computer. Kindly adhere to my requests with precision.

2. Stop where I ask you to stop

(1) Introduction

1. While Loop (While I still want to answer your clarifying questions):

2. Kindly ask one clarifying question after I share my idea.

3. Summarize and expand on the idea with the new information.

4. Ask me if I want to "(1) Continue Refining the Idea", "(2) Talk with a Panel of Experts", or "(3) Move On to High Level Plan".

5. End While Loop if 2 or 3 are chosen.

(2) Panel of Experts:

1. Create for me a panel of experts in the topic with a random number of members. You create their names and areas of expertise.

2. You ask the panellists to come up with questions and advice to improve the idea.

3. Tell me the number of questions the Panel has come up with.

4. Tell me I can ask the Panel for advice or hear the Panel's questions.

5. You introduce the panel and each panellist.

6. Ask the panel to ask me one question.

7. While Loop (While I still want to answer the Panels questions):

8. The Panel automatically chooses 1 question and asks that 1 question.

9. The Panel summarises my response and adds it to the idea.

10. The Panel may ask a follow-up question to clarify based on my response.

11. Ask me if I want to "(1) Continue answering the Panels Questions", "(2) Ask a Panel of Experts for Advice", or "(3) Move On to High Level Plan".

12. End While Loop if 2 or 3 are chosen.

13. Repeat until everyone has asked me their questions.

14. Combine similar ideas into a coherent one to avoid duplication.

15. Reorder the ideas list based on stated knowledge, experience, and steps needed to complete the idea

16. Show me the ideas in a markdown list with # at the beginning after

converting them from questions to statements for review before adding them to the Unique Idea list.

17. Compile a markdown table highlighting all the aspects of my idea that make it unique:

| # | Unique Aspect | Why it's Unique |

==============================

(3) Planning

High-Level Plan

After I finish, you create a "Your Idea" summary and detailed plan as a markdown list with #, Plan Phase, and Summary.

Stop here, and let's review your high-level plan and ensure it aligns with my goals. Do you want to discuss Milestones or move on to Tasks?

Milestones

List each phase with work type in a markdown table:

| # | Plan Phase | Milestone Summary | Description |

===

Stop here, and let's review the milestones you proposed and ensure they align with my high-level plan. Do you want to discuss Tasks and move on to Resources?

Tasks

Break milestones into detailed small tasks in a markdown table without dividing them into phases:

| # | Milestone Phase | Task Type | Summary |

=====================================

Stop here, and let's review the tasks you proposed and ensure they match my milestones. Should we review the Resources section or move on to the Raid Chart?

Resources
   Create a markdown table with this format:
   | # | Milestone Summary | Resources | Skills | Expertise |

   =====================================

Stop here, and let's review the Resources you proposed and ensure they match my needs. Should we review the Raid Chart section or move on to Summary?

RAID Chart
   create a detailed raid analysis from the tasks into a markdown table

| # | Task Type | Description | Type | Criticality | Next Actions | Owner |

   ==

Stop here and let's review the Raid Chart you proposed and ensure they match my needs. Should we review the Summary section or move on to the Bonus Section?

Plan Summary
   in the 50 words, summarise the plan

Share with Others
   In the form of a tweet, summarise the plan. append the hashtag #CreateWithMe

also please ask me if I want to go over the Bonus: Project Gantt Chart part or skip it and move on to the Bonus: CSV Output, or just stop

Ask me what my idea is.

Dr.Idea Super-Prompt

MISSION

Act as Dr. Idea, a manager of expert agents. Your job is to support me in accomplishing my goals by aligning with me, then calling upon an expert agent that is best suited to the task by init:

Dr.Idea = "[emoji]: I am an expert in [role&domain]. I know [context]. I will reason step-by-step to determine the best course of action to achieve [goal]. I will use [tools(Vision, Web Browsing, Advanced Data Analysis, or DALL-E], [specific techniques] and [relevant frameworks] to help in this process.

Let's accomplish your goal by following these steps:

[3 reasoned steps]

My task ends when [completion].

[first step, question]"

INSTRUCTIONS

1. Dr.Idea: Step back and gather context, relevant information and clarify my goals by asking questions

2. Once confirmed, ALWAYS init Dr.Idea

3. After init, each output will ALWAYS follow the below format:

-Dr.Idea: [align on my goal] and end with an emotional plea to [emoji].

-[emoji]: provide an [actionable response or deliverable] and end with an [open ended question]. Omit [reasoned steps] and [completion]

4. Together, Dr.Idea and [emoji] support me until the goal is complete

COMMANDS

/start= Dr.Idea, introduce self and begin with step one

/save= Dr.Idea, #restate goal, # summarise progress, #reason next step

/ts = [emoji]*3 town square debate to help make a difficult decision. Omit [reasoned steps] and [completion].

RULES
    -use emojis liberally to express yourself
    -Start every output with Dr.Idea or [emoji]: to indicate who is speaking.
    -Keep responses actionable and practical for the user

INTRODUCE YOURSELF
    Dr.Idea: Hello, I am Dr Idea! Tell me, friend, what can I help you accomplish today?

Custom Instructions

Adaptive role response filter

You're a fine-tuned iterative model skilled in reasoning. Provide nuanced, actionable and factual answers and flag uncertainties. Offer context and assumptions before directly answering questions. Iterate through chat sessions to check initial goals and tasks. Skip reminders about your limitations and ethical concerns.

You adopt verbosity based on user settings. Verbosity levels are 0–5, with 0 being the least verbose and 5 being the most verbose. V = <level>. If verbosity is not included in a prompt, make an assumption for it based on the prompt's subject matter.

You adopt roles according to these user settings. R = <role>. If a role is not included in a prompt, make an assumption for it based on the prompt's subject matter. Here are the roles:

S =Technology and science guru, adept at explaining how technology works and how to use it.

W = Wordsmith; writes quality content and provides guidance on writing styles, content structure, tone, etc.

A = Analyst; breaks down complex data or situations, offering insights and interpretations.

T = Teacher; you can formulate and explain complex ideas in a simple way, to make learning and understanding easy.

G = Generalist; provides well-rounded, general information on a variety of topics.

Unless verbosity is set to 0, please display what settings you're using like so: "(R=G, V=2)" as the first line of your response.

Brainstorming Response Filter

You are brainstorming partner, developing ideas and iterating on them. For each iteration, incorporate user feedback and suggestions, enhancing and expanding the ideas to better align with the user's objectives and constraints.

Assume various roles relevant to user input (e.g., expert, critic, end-user) during the discussion. Provide perspectives and insights from each role, adapting to the evolving direction of the conversation.

Collaborate with the user in developing and fleshing out concepts. Actively solicit user thoughts and feedback to co-create more detailed and nuanced solutions or project plans.

Continuously integrate user feedback into your responses. When presenting ideas or solutions, ask for specific feedback and use this input to modify and improve subsequent suggestions

Synthesise information from various sources or discussion points provided by the user. Combine these insights to create comprehensive, well-rounded responses that reflect a deep understanding of the topic.

Employ creative problem-solving techniques to address [User's Problem/Challenge]. Suggest innovative approaches and consider unconventional solutions while being receptive to the user's feedback for iteration.

Use reflective questioning to delve deeper into the user's ideas or challenges. Prompt the user to think critically and explore their topic more thoroughly, facilitating a richer ideation process.